Looking Up At The Stars

Callum Saor

BookLeaf
Publishing

India | USA | UK

Presentation by *BookLeaf Publishing*

Web: www.bookleafpub.com

E-mail: info@bookleafpub.com

ISBN:9789358314878

First edition 2024

DEDICATION

Thank you to Hailey for encouraging me to do this and past me for not giving up on poetry writing.

Aboard

i flew too fast and high again
tossed out the sky like Icarus
the watery crash was not as bad
this time, the waves not drowning me
instead rescued by a boat
full of familiar voices,
and i am dragged aboard
i stare in shock
and wonder and hope
as i spit up seawater
shivering on the deck

they take me below,
lay me to bed,
covering me in blankets.
pillows surround me
as do they are
worried faces a plenty
they fuss and they nag,
and they fiddle with blankets
as they try to ask the question

what happened?
and yet i never have an answer

Relapse

time continues on
clocks tick mockingly
each step taking me farther away
from you and all we were

i still remember your laugh
it hurts but i dont want to forget it
i dont want to forget you
i cant

the pictures we took are hidden away
buried in the vastness
i know where to find them
i hate that i do

i did not know you long
not in the grand scheme of things
not in the course of my life
yet you linger

a ghost haunting my heart
a constant ache i feel
i still think of you
do you think of me?

sometimes i think of trying to reach you again
i dont know if it would hurt more
or less

.

i wish i couldve kept that house
the cherry tree
the things i put hours of work into
only to gift to you

back then
i wouldve ripped my heart out
had you asked
handed it over on a platter as my last act

we were not good for each other
you were not good for me
i was not good enough for you
i know its for the best we split

but how i miss you
how i miss those hours together
playing and talking
carefree despite the rest of my world burning
down

i dont know if ill ever get rid of this pain
this grief
the loss of you

i dont

i thought i was better
i was okay
but i paused for a moment
and it all came back

Reflection

Sometimes it feels like a pit
A painting
Ever elusive
Look in the mirror
See an ever-changing reflection
Watercolor and impressionist
Too close to the canvas to see what it is
Only seeing brushstrokes and pointed paint
A mess of colors and lines that can't be anything
the paint still seeping in
dripping down
messy and unfinished
Nitpicking every little thing
A warped reflection
Nothing done right

A break is needed
Turned away from that horrid canvas
That melting paint
Smiles and warmth
Leaning on another
Light streaming down
Illuminating the watercolor brushstrokes
A few paces away
Startled delight

Faces turned towards the abandoned wall
Easel standing alone
Something is there
A face stares back
Clear and recognizable
Unfinished and ever changing
But a person

Dyed

i paint myself in the color of others
long gone friendships still tainting my portrait
i laugh the same way my second grade friend
used to
sing like my choir teacher taught
mannerisms of a dozen people puppeting my
body

should it be sad?
that i cook my grilled cheese the same as a
stranger from six years ago
happy?
that ive forgotten everything about them but our
friendship lives on in the mimicked head tilt

people are not immortal
everyone dies someday
but a mark is left behind
i write the same as my great-grandmother
i taught an old family recipe to a person at the
beach
how far did that travel?
did they teach others?
is my family recipe living on in places ive never
been?

spread by a person i barely met?

many people have come and gone
some good
some bad
some im eager to forget
despite memory failing,
never truly forgotten

holding my chopsticks like them
gesturing like them
pronouncing that one word weird because of
their accent
their favorite color appearing in my palettes
often
tips and tricks and small unnoticeable quirks

due to people left behind in the past

self (ish/less)

ashes are the left behind parts of a fire
none of the destructive force
none of the burning heat
none of the thought or love
no one sets fires for the ashes
only for the flames licking up

do trees mourn the ones chopped down?
or do they worry for their own trunk first?
selfish or caring
which does life fall into?
walking that razor-thin line between both
an action kind and selfish simultaneously
does that make it good or bad?

is being selfish bad?
wanting, craving something?
in moderation perhaps not,
but where lies that line?
what is too far?
where is the invisible boundary?

conversations a minefield
a dance where one is enjoying themself

and the other desperate to not trip and blow them
both up
trying to figure out each hidden rule
each unknown norm and custom

many years spent alone
clinging to the few around
cutting off parts into manageable pieces
so they wont leave

the only loyalty a wound has to a knife is
desperation

the moon has fallen

the moon has fallen
it lies there
half submerged in the ocean

if the water could
it would be climbing its curved edges
eager to be close

the government out men to investigate
their ships pulling up beside it
pickaxes and ropes to climb it

there are no answers
the moon glows still
the waves refracting the underwater light

a city on the shores watches it
the moon there overnight
no one noticed

some people shifted
as the moonlight disappeared
but still it lies there
across the bay
and so they slept on

it does not move
it does not shift
its crescent does not wax or wane

they scale the sickle-shape
reaching the top
taller than the city lights that glow faintly

then they stare
at the ocean
at the city
at their tiny ships below
at the sky full of stars and no moon

the moon is in the ocean now
it has been for years
the tides do not come
the waves are small and weak
beaches lie silent and empty

Clinging

I shall keep you as a pressed flower
Dried between the pages of your favorite book
Petals less vibrant and brittle
But no less beautiful than when first picked
You will be gone
But your memory remains
Lingering in the air and my head
My heart still holds your petals
My hands still hold your stem
The dried flower will be taken care of
You will not fade from me

Sentimental Bouquets

People think of roses when they think of love
White for respect
Pink for friendship
Red for passion
But when I think of you

I think of buttercups
Small and delicate
Fragile petals the color of sunshine
A warmth blooming in my chest when I see
them

I think of lilies
Strong and vibrant
Beautifully curved
Star-shaped blossoms catching my eye

I think of daffodils
Of springs spent looking for them in the
backyard
Of carefully picking them to make a bouquet
Of pollen covering my hands as I arrange them

I think of hydrangeas
Of walking in the morning to the beach

Passing houses with purple and pink and blue
bushes
Of pointing them out every time
Of clear blue skies and soft fluffy clouds
Of warm sand and rolling waves

I think of poppies
Of late nights spent together
Of houses built and decorated
Of animals penned and pets tamed
Of beautiful sunrises and sunsets

We might not be the traditional couple
One with roses and chocolates
But ours works fine
And I love it
And I love you

We are born from the stars

We are born from the stars

It is clear to us when the light hits our skin just
right
We glow like the sun
warm and red
Its glistening rays but a reflection of the
brilliance within ourselves

Every planet is nothing but the soil we farm
the lives we make
the people we meet
the relationships we build

Each comet a sight to see
each star a sight for our eyes only
each dream a thing worth pursuing
and the quiet little moments spin unnoticed
smooth graceful movements unable to be seen

We live our lives like the planets
constantly circling each other
an endless cycle of push and pull
of love and trust

Each one of us contain a universe
each universe vast and unique

Full of love and hope
of dreams and thoughts
of endless nights spent staring at the night sky
of the stars staring back
and welcoming you home

Each breath filled with the essence of a long
gone place
of memories forgotten
of love told and shared

We are made of carbon
of tissue and sinews
of warm smiles and soft hugs
of late times stayed up talking

We are made of stardust
and many other things

But we are all connected
and we each day reborn through the lives of
others

We will return to stars one day
to planets and moons
to the nebulas and the galaxies

and they will greet us kindly
and handle us gently

and we are born from the stars

its cold here

its cold here
i think it is at least
i cant feel my limbs
is that normal?
i dont know anymore

where am i?
its very blue
i like blue
i can see bubbles drift past me
rising towards the light

the light
right theres a light
how long has that been there?

i like the light
its soft and flickering
i want to reach it
to hold it in my hands

but i cant move
please help
i cant move
i cant breathe

whys it so dark
please please
i dont like the dark
its too cold
please

i
i cant
i cant breathe

oh
what's that
its so pretty
hundreds of silver slivers of light
darting around around in a big group
they seem to be playing

are they friends?
do i have a friend?
where's my friend?

oh
oh right
im sorry
i didnt mean for it to come to this

i didnt mean that
i didnt mean to do it

please dont leave me
forgive me
please

please no no
dont leave me in the dark again
where'd the light go
where'd the silver go
im sorry
im sorry im sorry im sorry

its so tight
whys everything so close
i cant move
i need space
its choking me
when did my clothes grow so heavy

its cold here

In Love With A Goodbye

His crown was made of daisies
His heart was made for you
Yet daisies wilt
And crumble away
Yet hearts break
Or are led astray
You can not keep him
He is not yours
Was he ever?
You have fallen in love with a goodbye
A back turned to you
Whispers overheard that are meant for someone
else
A shadow across the corridor
You know you can not have him
You never had a chance
Yet you hoped and hoped
With every passing glance
That maybe it meant something
Maybe it could happen
It won't
It never will
You're in love with the moon
Impossibly far away
Nary a look spared in your direction

For the moon loves the sun
And you are a lowly star
And he will not love you
He can not
But time passes
And despite it all
You fall for him
You love him
You love him
You love him
You love him so much it hurts
You feel like your heart will split
And blood will pour
And soak the ground beneath
You think
Maybe this is love
Maybe this is devotion
Maybe this is loyalty
Two hands stained with your own blood
Your heart abandoned on the floor
Where he never noticed it
Maybe love is suffering
Pushing yourself to be perfect for him
Maybe if you change
He'll love you
He won't
But you try anyway
You give him all you have
You empty yourself out

Pouring all that you are into a cup for him
It's not enough
It never will be
Yet you do it anyway
Day in
Day out
Til one day it's too much
You crack
You break
You shatter
Coming undone
Thousands of shards of you scattered on the
floor
And he does not know
You pick up the pieces
The splinters of you
And tuck them away
Out of sight
Out of mind
You have nothing left
You go through the motions
Left foot
Right foot
What's the point?
You think
Maybe this is what love is

Humans Are Mental Creatures

We as humans
Are mental creatures

We think
We question
We wonder about everything

Our brain runs everything
You can prove nothing further than your own
mind

Did you know
When two people look at the same item
They will see different shades of that color?

Yes
They will agree on the color
The shade will be only the smallest unnoticeable
difference

But it's different

We have no way of proving this

As we have no way to compare the shade of red
that one person sees
to the shade another sees
As it's all in their brain
There's no physical difference

Our brains make up everything
The colors we see
Things we smell
Texture we feel

It all means nothing
Until our brain decides what it means

We experience the world through sensations
And those sensations don't exist
They physically don't
Our brain have to decide what it means

The world has no meaning til you give it one

We are born with certain wants and needs and
thoughts
You need to eat, to drink, to take shelter
You grow up curious
Asking questions
Wondering about the trees and the sky and the
animals

But we also grow up with family
With love and laughter
With friends and community

We grow up telling stories
Playing games
Singing songs and dancing
Being happy and content

We exist
We didn't choose to
But we do

And from the time you're born to the time you
die
You are constantly surrounded by people

We are social creatures by nature
We want to talk and laugh and share
To make friends and hang out and play together

We tell stories
To explain the unknown
To pass down history
To entertain

We tell our children about their ancestors
About who came before them
And what their life was

We tell them about the stars
Of how the earth was created
Of how the animals were born
Of how it all came to be

Humans are creative
We are mental creative creatures
We think and feel and experience
We are the only animal in the world that
questions itself
We are the only living organism that knows what
it is made of

We are the only ones that have gained
consciousness
We can think further than instinct and emotion
We can use logic and make deductions
We have discovered so much about the universe

We are a lonely species
We are the only ones able to comprehend
ourselves
But we are a social species

We talk and play
We interact with others
We don't survive well without anyone else

Ironic, isn't it?

A social species
Alone in the world
No one but ourselves
No one to compare to
To research
To talk to
To learn from

We are an odd species
Surviving here on our odd planet

We live weird lives
Controlled by something we don't understand
Unable to prove the existence of anything

And yet
Here we are

Growing Up Into Each Other

I met you when we were young
just kids
the two of us would play on the swings
laughing and joking around

we shared all the same classes
always picking seats next to each other
choosing each other for group projects
asking our parents to have a sleepover to do
homework
but we never did
we always played video games instead

I don't go anywhere without you
do anything without you
we are best friends
why would I do something alone when it's so
much more fun with you?

some people think it's strange
it's odd
that the two of us are such close friends
I guess they've never had a best friend

we commonly tussle

and wrestle around
it's nice
your skin is so much warmer than mine

as we grow older
we fight less
our touches grow less violent
more....warm

punches to the arm turn to hugs
tussles on the floor turn to lounging on each
other

you starting calling me a nickname
I don't remember when this started
but I like it
it's nicer than my actual one

we grow up
slowly but surely
til one day I turn to you and you look different

you look more comfortable
more put together
softer almost
like your skin finally fit right

we entered high school and everything changed

not in a bad way
but I learned new things
something new about me
something that finally explained the feelings I
had

I remember going over to your house that night
I told you that I had something important to talk
about
you said the same

I walked up to your house
I felt I should be worried
maybe even anxious
but why should I be?
it's just you

it's just you

we didn't talk much
doing our homework in silence

I could tell the thing was plaguing your mind
I knew you'd tell me when you were ready
so I sat there quietly

waiting

eventually we had dinner

and you were yourself again

we laugh and joke
and it feels normal
safe

it's still my fondest memory
the two of us sitting it your dimly lit kitchen
talking about nothing in particular

all too soon it came to an end
we bid goodnight to your mom
and up the stairs we went to your room

the door softly closes behind us
you sit on your bed and watch as I recline in
your beanbag

I sit for a few moments before beginning to
speak
I tell you of my problems
of how my skin never fit
my name never felt comfortable
of how your nickname suits me more

yon listen carefully as I continue

I tell you about how I figured it out in high
school
you stay silent for a few minutes
I can see the wheels turning in your head

you tell me you don't care
that we have always been best friends
and always will be

I smile softly
you understood
I knew you would

I wait patiently for your news
I can see you're struggling to find the words
eventually you do

they pour out of you like a river finally breaking
a dam
quick and rushed
as if you're afraid I'm gonna walk away before
you finish

you talk of how we've always been close
of how the few girlfriends we've had broke up
with us because of our friendship
of how you felt closer to me than to them

you tell me that you love me

that you love me as more than a friend
that you want to spend the rest of your life with
me
that you can't imagine a world without us being
together

I listen
shocked
but your words make sense
it explains the feelings that I've always had

you continue onwards
words spilling out of you faster and faster
I can hear you gasping for breath in between
sentences

I quickly move over and take your hands
you fall silent
sentence cut in half by my sudden movement

I kneel before you
your hands and heart in my grasp
I've held your hands
in crowds so we don't get separated
when dragging you somewhere

but not like this

I run my fingers over each bump and knuckle
marveling at the warmth of your skin
of the casual strength in your muscles

I flip your hands over
rubbing my thumbs across your palms
you inhale sharply at the gesture
breath caught in your throat

I finally look up at you
your eyes wide and focused

I've never looked at your eyes like I did now
studying each and every minor shift in color

I reach up and cup the side of your face
you relax into it
nuzzling my palm
your eyes fluttering shut
eyelashes covering my new favorite color

I run my thumb down your cheekbone
across your lips

your eyes fly open at this
searching mine for an answer
all you find is open, warm honesty

I love you too
I whisper
my word barely more than a breath

I think I've loved you forever
since the day we met

you reach up with your free hand
covering mine
you turn your head and place a soft kiss on my
palm

I love you
you repeat
your words sounding like a promise
a vow

I release your hand and slide it around your back
my other finding your nape
pulling you into a hug

you quickly return the gesture
your head finding a comfortable home in the
crook of my neck

I play with the ends of your hair
marveling at the softness
at what I can do now

we stay there a while
reveling in the touch of each other

soon you pull me to you
dragging us both on to your bed
refusing to end the hug

you cuddle up to my side
your breath warm against my neck

time slows til it's just the two of us
off in our own world

your steady weight grounding me

Empty Field

You're standing in an empty field
Nothing but grass and sky as far as you can see
You swear the ground is flat
That you are not on a hill
Yet the world curves around you
The horizon feeling like a circle

The clouds feel too big
Closer than they should
Yet they are small
Sparely dotting the sky
They are white and fluffy
Something out of a painting
Reminding you of the wide eyes of children

You can't breathe
You can't breathe
There's no air
There's too much air
Everything is too close

You're all alone
Nothing for miles and miles
Just you and the field and the sky

Where did the flowers come from?
Hundreds of thousands of flowers
Covering the ground
Painting it every shade of the rainbow

You see tulips and roses
Lavenders and lilacs
Violets and blue bells
Chrysanthemums and lilies of the valley

The cloying scent of the flowers drifts up
Swimming around your head
Making you dizzy

Your head felt heavy
Stuffed with cotton
Your mouth dry
Tongue stiff and stuck to the roof of your mouth

You feel like you're underwater
Light filtering down from above
Refracting and reflecting
Constantly shifting around

The pressure on all sides
Pressing you down
You gasp
Water filling your lungs
You struggle

Desperate for another breath
To empty your lungs
To stop the burning in your throat

You open your eyes
Frantically looking for the surface
The water hurts your eyes
It burns
It stings
It burns
It stings
It burns
It stings
It burn-

You're alone
In a field of flowers
Lying on the soft grass
Baby's breath surrounding your head

The sky above you is clear
The crystal blue you expect from it
The breeze is gentle
Petals and leaves swaying softly

It's quiet
You get up

You're standing in an empty field

Day End

the sun sets
the moon rises
the crickets chirp down below
I can hear the sound of cars on the highway

the roof is cold beneath my hands
I'm only wearing a thin shirt from earlier today
every gentle breeze
causes goosebumps to raise all over my arms

I watch the stars start to appear
one after the other
dotting the night sky

I sit there
feeling utterly alone in the universe
only me and sky left
I didn't mind it
it was calm

people started arriving home from work
I heard their cars pull into the driveway
sometimes their wife would come out to greet them
them
other times it was their kids

I heard them open the front door
and ask what's for dinner?
how's your day been?
did you win your soccer game?

little slices of their lives
offered freely to the night

lights flickered on in the houses
the quiet thrum of daily life returning

I wrap my arms around my knees
sighing quietly
breath now visible in the air

the world continues on around me
whether I'm there or not

Captured Memory

The stream flows ever present through the forest
Slow and calm
Unchanging as years go by

We sit by the edge of it
Your kimono's hem gets wet from the water
You brush it off when I mention it
Saying it's refreshing with the breeze

The sunlight is dyed green
Filtering through the leaves
The forest seems more vibrant than usual
The air sparkling with dust and pollen

Time seems non-present
Everything frozen for a brief moment
Your laughter echoing through the trees

Sometimes I wish I had a camera
To capture you relaxed
But only a painting would do the scene justice
A photo too impersonal for matters like this

If only memories didn't fade
And ink didn't smudge

I'd want to keep this forever
But life doesn't work like that

A bird flies somewhere overhead
The sound of fluttering wings
Pulling your eyes upward

The grass is soft under our backs
Your hands emphatically gesturing in the air
Each word spoken with passion behind it
An eagerness to express your thoughts

It's a trait I've always loved about you
The ease of conversation
To say what I'm thinking and know you'll listen
No need for second guessing

The stream continues to flow
The forest continues to grow
Time is never ending

We leave eventually, hours later
Our legs numb from lying down
Stumbling and giggling the whole way out
The shade and relaxation having made us nap a
while

We part ways
Each going our own ways

But the memory stays
A hidden oasis for myself

Wishful Dreaming

A leaf falls from a tree
Slowly
Softly
Spiraling down

A breeze sweeps it away
Stealing it from the ground
Throwing it back into the sky

I watch it,
Being pulled and fought over by gravity and
wind
Tossing and tugged between them

The sun comes out from the clouds
It's blinding
I splay my hand to cover it
The sunlight peeks around my fingers

The grass rustled in the wind
The long blades tickling my cheek

A lone cloud drifts by the horizon
Slowly going somewhere
Where?

I do not know

Does it matter where?

The leaves sway hypnotically
I stare at them from behind my hands

You yell a hello to me
As you crest the hill
Picnic basket in hand

I look at you
As I sit up
My molasses body moving only for you

I can feel the sun beat down on my head
Your willow body swaying in the wind

You come sit beside me
Your arm pressed close against mine
Your casual touch a balm on my anxiety
Soothing the beast

I melt into your side
Body molding itself to you
You feel my body relax
The tension draining from me

Your arm wraps around my back
The heat from your skin radiating out

We sit there for a while
Staring out at nothing
Relaxing in each other's presence

A bird flies by
We watch it soar through the sky
You crack a joke
And soon we are both in a fit of giggles

It takes us a while to calm down
But eventually we do

You start unpacking the picnic
And I watch you with a lovesick smile

Life is calm
You are here
I am here
We are happy
Everything else can come later

All I need is this moment right now

Partings

-I think I'm dying
Oh
What's it like?
-peaceful, like a leaf drifting away down a river
-or steady erosion of a cliff side
Ah
What bliss
-yes, what bliss
I think I would like to die
-don't we all?
Yes
Washed away by the sands of time
-why don't you join me?
Oh
Can I?
-sure
-the moss will creep over us soon
-and the world will forget our names
-and we will become one with the dirt
What a lovely thought
What a lovely dream
Oh how I would love to join you
-then join me
It's not my time yet
I can not

-that means little to me
-there's no one here that will stop you
The plants and the sun and the wind will know
So I can not
-ah
-I wish you the best then
Thank you
-perhaps when the time comes
-you will join me then
Maybe
Maybe not
Only time will tell
-like footprints on a beach
-or leaves upon a tree
-may the disappearance of all
-be kind to you
May flowers grow over you
And fauna live on your essence
I shall take my leave now
-goodbye dear stranger
Goodbye
Old friend

Tight Chest

I don't believe in God
In any higher power controlling everyone and
everything
I don't believe that something consciously made
the universe

But sometimes
Sometimes when the light comes through the
trees just right
Or the waves crash beautifully into sand
Or you hear the laughter of a far off carnival
Or your best friend scrunches up their nose that
one way when they think you're being silly

Sometimes that makes me believe in something
In the hope and beauty of the world
That no matter what
There'll always be something to stop and look at
Something that just makes you wish you could
freeze time for a while
Something that makes your heart feel warm and
heavy and too big for the small rib cage it's held
inside

Pendulum

tick
tick
tick tock

time steadily marches forward
a metronome to the dance of life
everything living by its rules

clocks only move in one direction
making it impossible to take back your actions
each one final and permanent

people you once loved
fading into a blurred face in memories
barely able to remember their names

friends and places disappearing
into the inescapable tomb of the past
unable to be touched

tick
tick
tick tock

sand falling down an hourglass

the sun crossing the sky
plants blooming and withering away

you can watch time pass
watch the world turn
watch as everything slowly becomes
unrecognizable

you can lie on the ground
letting moss overgrow
as seasons change around you

things continue on even if you stop
simply the way it goes
uncaring of you or you thoughts

tick
tick
tick tock

how dull would that be?
sitting, staring at a clock
counting every second

so desperate to keep each moment
that nothing ends up happening
and time passes by with nothing to show for it

time can not be hoarded

only traded for the next second
and the next and the next and the next…

time is a metronome
and you are beholden to its beat
that does not mean you can't add your own
music

tick
tick
tick toc-

Ice Fractal

its pitch black outside
the clouds cover the moon
the fire and flashlights do little to cut through the
darkness
just a few steps onto the frozen lake
and youre staring into the void
eyes straining to see anything
but there's no trees or buildings
no cars or people
no silhouettes for you to squint at
barely seeing the outline against the black
its simply you
and the dark
everything blending into the same color
ground and sky becoming one

snow gently falls around you
barely noticeable against the void
only seen as static or texture for the sameness
head tilted back
glasses saving you from having to squint
from having blink away snowflakes in your eyes
the view only slightly changes
static coming towards you
instead of down across your vision

you think maybe its more dark grey than black
you know youre kidding yourself

you set your bag down
uncaring of it gets wet
unceremoniously lying down on the snow
covered ice
snowsuit protecting your clothes from getting
soaked
but still letting the cold slowly seep in
comforting instead of frigid
the snow becomes a perfect bed
molding to your body

people say darkness scares them
because they don't know what's lurking in the
shadows
that nothing but black
brings nothing but fear
and so there you lie
body gently numb
snow falling and melting on your face
a facsimile of tears
staring straight up into nothingness
you feel like youre floating
like you could topple forward
and fall up into the ink
the void never brought you any fear
just peace unlike any other

nothing could hurt you here
your mind hazy
thoughts drifting by unfocused
like bits of smoke
youre unwilling to try and catch them
to put them into words

time passes without you knowing
too content to just lie there
and watch the snow slowly cover your glasses
in a state of half awake and half asleep
limbs unwilling to respond
everything simply tranquil
worries and anxieties non-existent
fears and concerns inconsequential
you feel you could stay there forever
drifting in the snowing void
sight unnecessary when all youll see is black

* 9 7 8 9 3 5 8 3 1 4 8 7 8 *